The Littlest Peanut

A Baby Book for the Teeny Tiny Ones

WELCOME BABY!

Written by Shannan Wilson

Illustrated by Joe Cuniff

The Littlest Peanut:
A Baby Book for the Teeny Tiny Ones

ISBN 978-0-692-46380-2
Library of Congress Control Number 2011931196

Printing in the United States.
10 9 8 7 6 5 4 3

The Littlest Peanut Publishing
www.TheLittlestPeanut.com

CPSIA facility code: BP 312812

To my littlest peanuts,
Kendall and Breckie.

In the words of Milton Berle,
"Laughter is an instant vacation."
Allow yourself to do so each day,
no matter how dark the days may
seem. Cheers to your little peanut,
may the tiny one grow and grow.

Note from the author, Shannan Wilson . . .

The Littlest Peanut began when my daughter was born at thirty-four weeks. It started off as a poem and then was put away when we brought her home three and a half weeks later. It wasn't until I had my second preemie, my son, born at thirty weeks, that the idea came back to me. There in the NICU, where I had just spent time eighteen months prior, were these tiny little babies fighting for their lives.

Some were stronger than others, some were crashing every hour and needed the constant care of a nurse, some were on their way out the door, but the stress in their parents' eyes and the look of utter fear mixed with pure hope were all the same.

We all have this bond, the parents of NICU babies. The small things that mean so much, like the blessed feeling of holding their little finger, changing a diaper, taking a temperature, or just watching them breathing and living through their closed Isolette.

It was with this intent that *The Littlest Peanut* was created: to journal these special moments and to keep track of their progress during this very confusing and hazy time.

This is my baby book, special for me.

To jot down your thoughts, and one day I'll see the challenges and obstacles I overcame with your prayers. This book will be something that one day we will share.

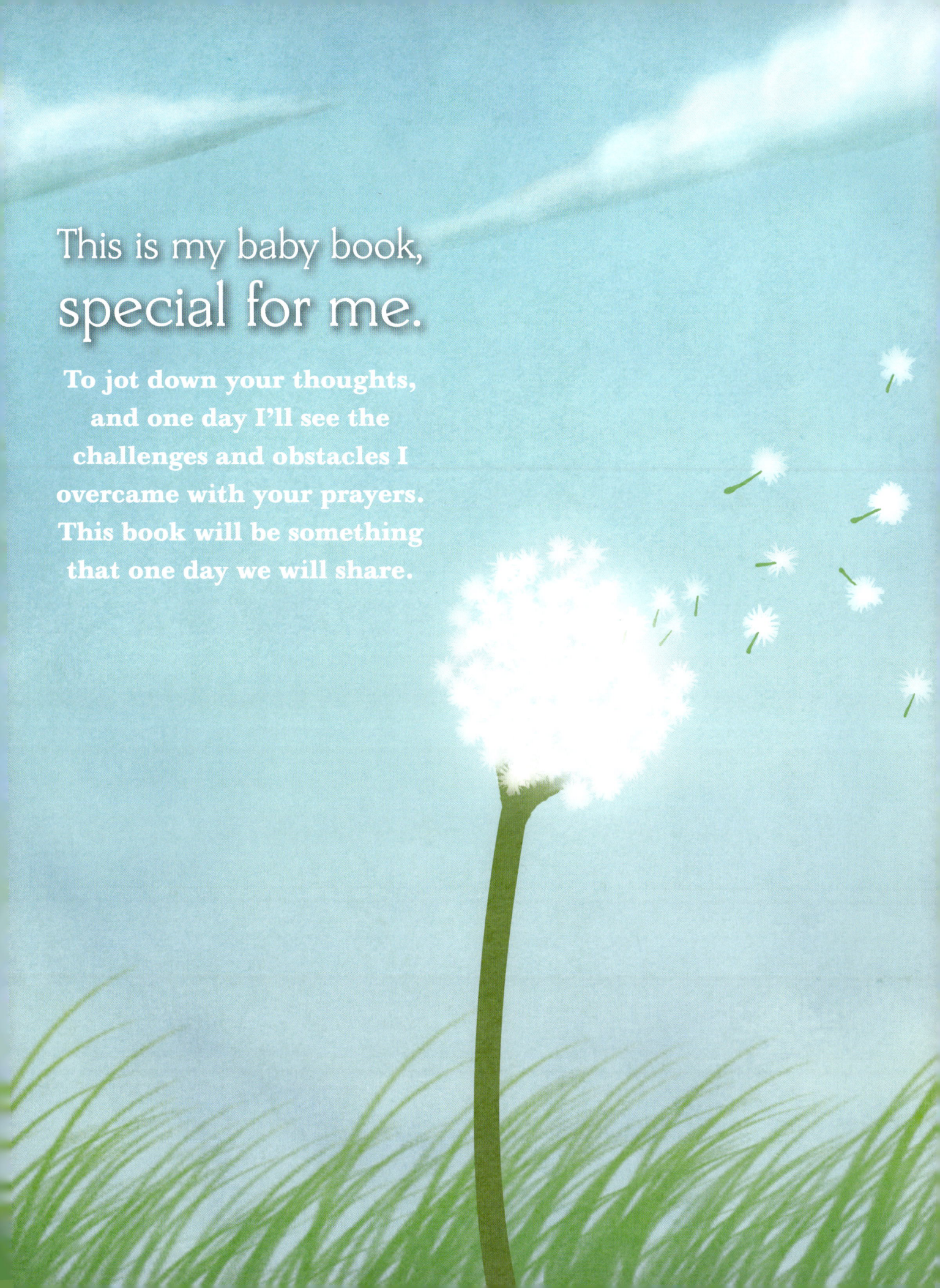

The Littlest Peanut

a prayer and a wish

Hello little peanut,
how I missed you through the night.

Hello my sweet thing,
I hope soon to hold you tight.

Every morning I awake with
positive thoughts for you.

Knowing that throughout the night
you grew, and grew, and grew.

The road ahead may be rocky,
but I see that you are strong.

The nurses have big plans for you;
they'll help us move along.

Oh, very soon we will take you home
because you're big and better.

We will tuck into your new cozy bed
and love you forever and ever.

My First Pictures

affix picture here

affix picture here

My First Days
on this Big Wide Earth!

My full name is: _____

My birthday is on: _____

My due date was on _____
but I surprised everyone and came _____weeks
_____day(s) early at _____ a.m. / p.m.

I weighed _____ lbs and _____ oz and was _____ inches _____ cm long.

I was born in _____
and was delivered by _____.
_____Doctor _____Nurse _____Mid-Wife _____Policeman

The color of my hair is _____ and my eyes are _____.

I think I look like _____.

My condition at birth was _____.
and my Apgar Score was _____.

My blood type is _____.

EXTRA! EXTRA!
MAJOR HEADLINES OF THE DAY

What is the most popular song?

_____

What is the most current concern in our country?

_____

_____

What is the most popular movie?

_____

What is the price of gas?

_____

What is the price of milk?

_____

How much do diapers cost?

_____

Affix a newspaper article here.

Journal

Each day in the NICU comes with challenges and fears, so keep track of your thoughts all right here. Use this space as your journal as your little peanut grows.

My first fighting days: _____

_____

_____

_____

_____

_____

_____

Everyone's wishes for me are: _____

_____

_____

_____

_____

_____

_____

_____

Have Laughter   Find Strength   Sleep Well

Journal

_____

_____

_____

_____

_____

_____

_____

_____

_____

_____

_____

_____

_____

_____

_____

_____

_____

_____

_____

_____

_____

Think in the Present   *Dream Happy*   *Attempt a Smile*

Journal

_____

_____

_____

_____

_____

_____

_____

_____

_____

_____

_____

_____

_____

_____

_____

_____

_____

_____

_____

_____

_____

Laugh and Cry   Breathe In   Feel Blessed

Journal

_____
_____
_____
_____
_____
_____
_____
_____
_____
_____
_____
_____
_____
_____
_____
_____
_____
_____
_____
_____
_____
_____

Take Walks   Get Rest   Dream Positive

Journal

_____
_____
_____
_____
_____
_____
_____
_____
_____
_____
_____
_____
_____
_____
_____
_____
_____
_____
_____
_____
_____

Love Yourself   Find Humor   Just Be

Medical Notes

When my medical team comes to see me, it is hard to remember all they say.
These pages are for you to take notes during these long and hazy days.

Important Tests/Results:

_____

_____

_____

_____

_____

_____

_____

_____

Positive Feedback
and Plans of Action:

_____

_____

_____

_____

_____

_____

_____

_____

_____

_____

_____

_____

Conversations with my Neonatologist:

_____

_____

_____

_____

_____

_____

_____

_____

Scans and Other Medical Information:

_____
_____
_____
_____
_____
_____
_____

How is my temperature maintaining?:

_____
_____
_____
_____
_____
_____
_____

Have I had jaundice and what have my bilirubin levels been?:

_____
_____
_____
_____
_____
_____

Respiratory Milestones

Challenges and accomplishments as I'm working to breathe.

I went off of the ventilator when: _____

I went off of the CPAP when: _____

I came off of all respiratory support when: _____

Other notes: _____

Feeding Schedule

I'm tiny but I love to eat!

What is my feeding schedule throughout each week? _____
_____
_____

First gavage feeding and how many mls: _____
_____

The first day I fed from a bottle: _____

My first time I latched to Mommy: _____
This was a tough one; latching is hard for our little mouths to do!

Challenges and accomplishments for feeding: _____
_____
_____

Did I experience apnea at all? _____

Was I sleepy during my feeds? _____

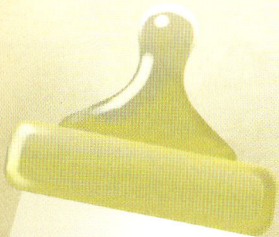

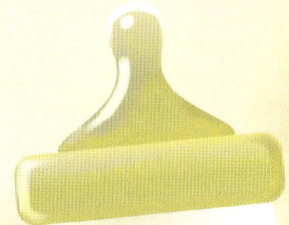

Me

The Family Tree

My Weight and Size

Every day while I sleep I grow a little more.
Keep track of my weight as I head toward the door!

AGE	WEIGHT	LENGTH	AGE	WEIGHT	LENGTH
1st Week	_____	_____	6th Week	_____	_____
2nd Week	_____	_____	7th Week	_____	_____
3rd Week	_____	_____	8th Week	_____	_____
4th Week	_____	_____	9th Week	_____	_____
5th Week	_____	_____	10th Week	_____	_____

AGE	WEIGHT	LENGTH
11th Week	_____	_____
12th Week	_____	_____
13th Week	_____	_____
14th Week	_____	_____
15th Week	_____	_____

AGE	WEIGHT	LENGTH
16th Week	_____	_____
17th Week	_____	_____
18th Week	_____	_____
19th Week	_____	_____
20th Week	_____	_____

Pictures and Artwork

From My Family and Loved Ones

My Visitors

name: _____ date: _____

name: _____ date: _____

name: _____ date: _____

name: _____ date: _____

name: _____ date: _____

name: _____ date: _____

name: _____ date: _____

name: _____ date: _____

name: _____ date: _____

name: _____ date: _____

name: _____ date: _____

name: _____ date: _____

name: _____ date: _____

name: _____ date: _____

My Gifts

name: _____ gift: _____

name: _____ gift: _____

name: _____ gift: _____

name: _____ gift: _____

name: _____ gift: _____

name: _____ gift: _____

name: _____ gift: _____

name: _____ gift: _____

name: _____ gift: _____

name: _____ gift: _____

name: _____ gift: _____

name: _____ gift: _____

name: _____ gift: _____

name: _____ gift: _____

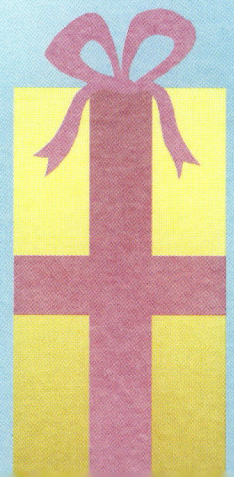

My Milestones

affix picture here

My first bath: _____

Mommy's first diaper change: _____

My first time in Mommy's arms: _____

My first time in Daddy's arms: _____

My neighbors in the NICU: _____

My first Kangaroo Care with Mommy: _____

My first little outfit that wasn't from the hospital: _____

My first night in my crib from my Isolette: _____

My favorite stuffed animal: _____

My Teeny Tiny Footprints

affix picture here

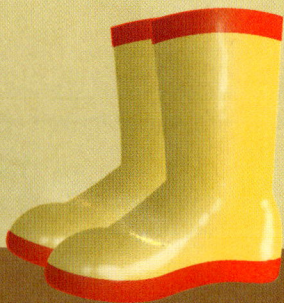

My Favorite Nurse is...

affix picture here

My Nicknames:

Funny Comments:

Artwork and Keepsakes
from My Nurses

Cards and Keepsakes